EXPLORERS

Lewis and Clark

Kristin Petrie

ABDO
Publishing Company

visit us at
www.abdopublishing.com

Published by ABDO Publishing Company, 4940 Viking Drive, Edina, Minnesota 55435.
Copyright © 2007 by Abdo Consulting Group, Inc. International copyrights reserved in all
countries. No part of this book may be reproduced in any form without written permission
from the publisher. The Checkerboard Library™ is a trademark and logo of ABDO Publishing
Company.

Printed in the United States.

Cover Photos: Corbis, North Wind
Interior Photos: Corbis pp. 5, 7, 9, 15, 17, 19, 21, 23, 27, 29; North Wind pp. 11, 13

Series Coordinator: Heidi M. Dahmes
Editors: Rochelle Baltzer, Heidi M. Dahmes
Art Direction & Cover Design: Neil Klinepier
Interior Design & Maps: Dave Bullen

Library of Congress Cataloging-in-Publication Data

Petrie, Kristin, 1970-
  Lewis and Clark / Kristin Petrie.
    p. cm. -- (Explorers)
  Includes index.
  ISBN-10 1-59679-743-6
  ISBN-13 978-1-59679-743-7
  1. Lewis and Clark Expedition (1804-1806)--Juvenile literature. 2. West (U.S.)--Discovery and
exploration--Juvenile literature. 3. West (U.S.)--Description and travel--Juvenile literature. 4.
Lewis, Meriwether, 1774-1809--Juvenile literature. 5. Clark, William, 1770-1838--Juvenile
literature. 6. Explorers--West (U.S.)--Biography--Juvenile literature. I. Title. II. Series.

F592.7.P48 2006
917.804'2--dc22

                                                                          2005017497

Contents

Lewis and Clark

Traversing wild rivers, riding dangerous **rapids**, climbing rugged mountains, and exploring unknown lands. Now that's adventure!

In 1804, Meriwether Lewis and William Clark **embarked** on this sort of exciting journey. They traveled the Missouri River from a point near St. Louis, Missouri, to present-day Montana. Continuing by land and by water, they eventually reached the Pacific Ocean.

President Thomas Jefferson hired Lewis and Clark for this expedition. The president wanted to know more about the land west of the Mississippi River.

For the voyage, Jefferson gave Lewis and Clark specific instructions. He told them to search for a water passage to the Pacific. He also wanted detailed accounts and maps of every observation. And, Lewis and Clark were to study and make friends with the Native Americans.

1271
Polo left for Asia

1295
Polo returned to Italy

1254
Marco Polo born

1275
Polo met Kublai Khan

Meriwether Lewis and William Clark were the first to explore the Missouri River from its mouth to its source.

The Lewis and Clark expedition was the first to cross America's unexplored West. It has been called the Voyage of Discovery. The results of this brave journey led to settlement of the West.

1460 or 1474
Juan Ponce de León born

1480
Ferdinand Magellan born

1324
Polo died

1475
Vasco Núñez de Balboa born

William Clark

Lewis and Clark are two names that seem to go together as one. You might think they were brothers! However, the two only crossed paths as adults.

William Clark was born on August 1, 1770, in Caroline County, Virginia. He was the ninth of John and Ann Roger Clark's ten children.

William grew up on a plantation. He loved the wide-open country. Although he had little formal schooling, William learned the skills expected of a Virginia gentleman. These included hunting, horseback riding, and managing an estate.

In 1784, the Clark family moved to Kentucky. William loved living on the frontier. He spent much of his time **foraging** through the woods.

William's older brother was a **Revolutionary War** hero. So growing up, William heard many tales about his brother's

1500
Balboa joined expedition to South America

1493
Ponce de León joined expedition to New World

1502
Ponce de León became governor of Higüey

William Clark

fearless feats. Not surprisingly, William joined the army when he was 21 years old.

For four years, William served along the Ohio and Indiana frontiers. He rose in rank to lieutenant. But in 1796, he left the army and returned to Kentucky. After the deaths of his parents, William inherited the family's home and land. And in 1803, he received an offer of adventure that he couldn't refuse.

1508
Ponce de León's first expedition

1514
Ponce de León knighted by King Ferdinand II

1513
Ponce de León's second expedition, discovered Florida and the Gulf Stream; Balboa was the first European to sight the Pacific Ocean

Meriwether Lewis

This exciting offer came from a man named Meriwether Lewis. Meriwether was born in Virginia on August 18, 1774, to William and Lucy Lewis. Meriwether had an older sister, Jane, and a younger brother, Reuben. The Lewis family lived on a plantation near Charlottesville.

Like many young boys, Meriwether loved adventure and the outdoors. He had a special interest in **geology**, as well as plant and animal life.

The Lewis family moved to Georgia when Meriwether was eight or nine. When he was 13, Meriwether returned to Virginia to begin formal schooling. He also learned how to manage his family's large plantation. The Lewises grew tobacco, corn, and wheat.

When Meriwether was 20 years old, he joined the army. During this time, he met and served with William Clark. The two young men established a lasting friendship.

1520
Magellan discovered the Strait of Magellan

1554
Walter Raleigh born

1519
Magellan led expedition to Spice Islands; Balboa died

1521
Ponce de León's third expedition, died in Cuba; Magellan died

Would You?

Would you be able to run a plantation? What tasks do you think Lewis performed for this job?

During his time in the army, Meriwether studied Native American languages and habits.

Assignment

By 1796, Lewis and Clark had gone their separate ways. But, one man would bring them back together. In 1801, Thomas Jefferson became president of the United States. Shortly thereafter, he made Lewis his personal secretary.

For years, Jefferson had dreamed of expanding America's frontier. He believed the Louisiana Territory was full of promise. At that time, Louisiana stretched from the Mississippi River to the Rocky Mountains. And, France was the proud owner of the region.

In 1803, the United States bought the land from France. President Jefferson was eager to learn more about the area. Because Lewis spent so much time with Jefferson, he was a natural choice for any special project. So, the president asked Lewis to lead an expedition to the Louisiana Territory. Lewis sent a letter to Clark, requesting his help.

1580
John Smith born

1585
Raleigh knighted by Queen Elizabeth I

1565
Henry Hudson born

1584–1589
Raleigh sponsored expeditions

Lewis and Clark had gained valuable knowledge during their time in the army. They had learned about wilderness survival while living on the border of civilization. And, rigid training had them in top physical condition. Their combined talents would make them perfect for this assignment.

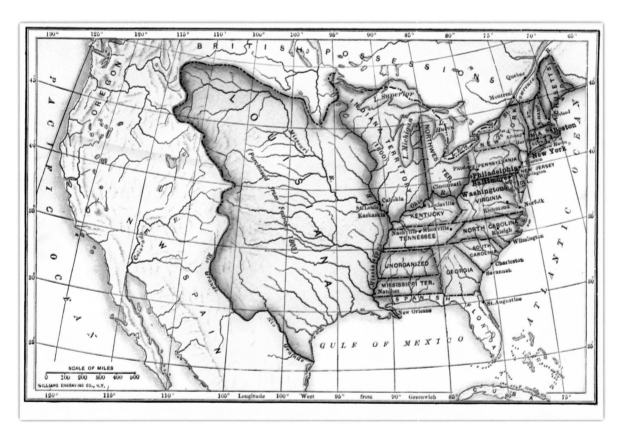

A map of the United States in 1803

Preparation

President Jefferson expected detailed information from Lewis and Clark about the Louisiana Territory. He wanted to know about the natives, the landscapes, the plants, and the wildlife.

Jefferson also wanted Lewis and Clark to search for a northwest passage. For centuries, explorers had been searching for this fabled waterway. They believed it crossed through North America and connected the Atlantic and Pacific oceans. If found, trade between North America and Asia would be easier.

To prepare Lewis for the demands of the journey, Jefferson sent him to Pennsylvania. There, scholars taught Lewis how to classify plants and animals. Lewis also learned how to navigate by observing the position of the stars.

1595
Raleigh led first expedition

1588
Raleigh helped defeat the Spanish Armada

1606
Smith joined expedition to North America

Would You?

Would you be excited to receive an assignment from the president? Do you think Lewis and Clark were nervous?

Following Jefferson's wishes, both Lewis and Clark kept detailed accounts of their expedition. Clark included many sketches in his journal entries.

The Corps

Lewis and Clark needed a good team to make this grand plan work. So, they **recruited** experienced woodsmen to guide the expedition. The explorers signed on skilled hunters to keep the group fed. And, they found soldiers to protect the men from dangers, such as hostile natives.

Lewis and Clark also hired temporary workers to move their heavy supply boat up the river. When recruitment was complete, the expedition numbered about 40 men. Lewis and Clark called their group the Corps of Discovery.

In December 1803, Lewis and Clark set up a training camp. Camp Dubois was located in Illinois, just 18 miles (29 km) north of St. Louis, Missouri. There, Clark trained the Corps for upcoming challenges.

During these cold months, Lewis made the final preparations. He gathered information about the area they would soon be exploring. He also secured the necessary supplies, equipment, and trade goods.

1607
Hudson's first expedition

1609
Hudson's third expedition

1608
Hudson's second expedition

1610–1611
Hudson's last expedition, he died

Would You?

Would you have the necessary skills to join an expedition like the one Lewis and Clark made?

Medical supplies similar to those used by the Corps are displayed at Lewis and Clark Heritage Days. This annual event takes place in St. Charles, Missouri. It celebrates the Lewis and Clark expedition.

1614
Smith led expedition to North America, charted and named New England

1616
Raleigh's second expedition

Wilderness

By early spring, Lewis and Clark were eager to begin their journey. The team pushed off the banks of the Missouri River on May 14, 1804. The explorers had one **keelboat** and two **pirogues**. The 55-foot (17-m) keelboat carried food, weapons, trade items, and scientific instruments. The pirogues carried most of the Corps members.

Soon after departing their camp, the men left civilization. They found the wilderness amazing and lively. They ate well, because the river was full of fish. Unfortunately, the mosquitoes made them miserable.

Progress was slow. The men pushed and pulled their heavy boats upstream for months. By September, the hardworking crew reached present-day South Dakota. There, herds of buffalo, elk, deer, and antelope thrilled Lewis.

Throughout the entire expedition, Lewis and Clark kept detailed journals of new sights and sounds. Many other Corps members also recorded their experiences.

1618	1637	1645
Raleigh died	Jacques Marquette born	Louis Jolliet born

1631	1643
Smith died	René-Robert Cavelier de La Salle born

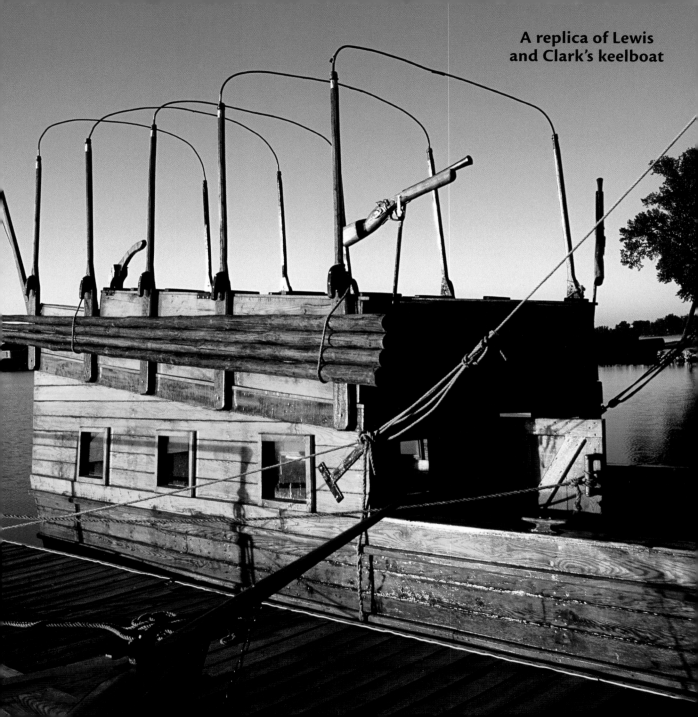

A replica of Lewis and Clark's keelboat

Natives

During the journey, the Corps encountered many Native American tribes. Lewis and Clark tried to establish friendly relations with the native peoples. They offered gifts in order to win over the natives. Then, they told the natives that the United States had bought the land they lived on.

Usually, the Corps's meetings were friendly. The natives often helped the voyagers and described what lay ahead. But, the Teton Sioux of South Dakota were wary of the explorers. Lewis and Clark left without becoming **allies** with this tribe.

By November, Lewis and Clark reached the Mandan and Hidatsa villages. These were near today's Bismarck, North Dakota. The Corps built a camp called Fort Mandan and settled there for the winter. By this point in the voyage, the Corps had traveled 1,600 miles (2,600 km).

Lewis and Clark learned as much as they could about the Mandan and Hidatsa tribes. Both tribes were friendly and interested in trading with the explorers.

1669
La Salle explored Ohio region

1666
La Salle sailed to Canada

1673
Marquette and Jolliet explored the Mississippi River

The Hidatsa lived in earth lodges similar to this one.

Onward!

The Corps grew during its time at Fort Mandan. Lewis and Clark hired a French-Canadian fur trapper named Toussaint Charbonneau as an interpreter. His wife Sacagawea also joined the expedition. She was a Native American of the Shoshone tribe. Sacagawea became a very important interpreter for the rest of the journey.

On April 7, 1805, Lewis and Clark waved good-bye to their Mandan and Hidatsa friends. Sixteen Corps members sailed the **keelboat** back down the Missouri River. The boat was loaded with reports, maps, and plant and land samples for President Jefferson.

Lewis and Clark led the rest of the Corps west on the Missouri. In present-day Montana, the **terrain** changed from lush to dry and rugged.

1675
Marquette died

1682
La Salle's second Mississippi River expedition

1679
La Salle's first Mississippi River expedition

In his journal, Lewis commented on the large numbers of buffalo that the group saw along the Great Plains.

In amazement, Lewis wrote about the huge numbers of animals that roamed the land. Many animals, such as bighorn sheep, were new to the explorers. In fact, the men encountered their first grizzly bears in Montana!

1687
La Salle died

1684
La Salle's third Mississippi River expedition

1700
Jolliet died

Before reaching the Rocky Mountains, the Corps faced its first major challenge. On June 13, the explorers encountered the Great Falls of the Missouri. The only way around the falls was to walk. So, the men hauled their boats and supplies around the falls. Nearly four weeks later, they returned to the Missouri.

On July 25, the expedition reached Three Forks. This is where three rivers join to form the Missouri. Lewis and Clark named these rivers the Madison, the Gallatin, and the Jefferson. They decided to follow the Jefferson River. This led them westward toward the mountains.

August provided a needed break. Lewis and Clark came upon the Shoshone Native Americans. To their luck, Chief Cameahwait was Sacagawea's brother. There was a joyful reunion. And, Sacagawea convinced Cameahwait to provide the expedition with horses, supplies, and a guide.

After leaving the Shoshone, the Corps continued through the Bitterroot Range of the Rocky Mountains. Travel was difficult, and there were few animals to kill for food. The

1770
William Clark born

1786
Sacagawea born

1774
Meriwether Lewis born

1800
Sacagawea captured

steep mountain trails caused many horses to fall. To make matters worse, winter storms hit in early September.

Eventually, the trails **descended** into a valley along the Clearwater River. Near today's Lewiston, Idaho, the Corps met Nez Percé Native Americans. This tribe helped the men build canoes, so the explorers could travel by water.

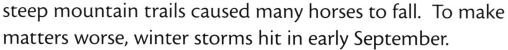

Two demonstrators make a dugout canoe

Pacific
Ocean

Fort Clatsop

Columbia River

Washington

R O C K Y

Montana

BITTERROOT RANGE

Clearwater River

Lewis's Return

Columbia River

Great Falls

Oregon

Snake River

Lemhi River

M O U N T A I N S

Three Forks

Yellowstone River

Clark's Return

Idaho

Jefferson River

Gallatin River

Madison River

Snake River

Wyoming

The Journeys of Lewis & Clark

1804 TO 1805 →

1806 →

CANADA

North
Dakota

Fort Mandan

*Missouri
River*

Minnesota

Mississippi River

Wisconsin

South
Dakota

*Missouri
River*

Nebraska

Iowa

Illinois

Missouri River

Kansas

Missouri

St. Louis

N

Homebound

The Corps members followed the Clearwater, Snake, and Columbia rivers to the Pacific Ocean. They arrived in early November 1805. The voyagers rejoiced, but they knew the journey was not over. They still had to get home.

Winter was approaching. So, the men built Fort Clatsop near present-day Astoria, Oregon. Lewis and Clark spent the rainy winter updating their journals and maps. The other voyagers made shoes and clothing for the return trip.

On March 23, 1806, the Corps set out once again. The challenges continued, but the group was more prepared this time.

Near today's Missoula, Montana, Lewis and Clark split the Corps into two groups. In this way, they hoped to investigate more of the wilderness. Lewis and his men took a shortcut that led to the Missouri. Clark and his group followed a more southerly route. They went down the Yellowstone River.

1804
Lewis and Clark began exploring the Pacific Northwest

1806
Lewis and Clark returned to Missouri

1805
Sacagawea joined the Lewis and Clark expedition

On August 12, the groups reunited on the Missouri River. Two days later, Lewis and Clark said good-bye to Sacagawea and her family. The Corps of Discovery reached St. Louis, Missouri, on September 23, 1806. The explorers received a lively welcome.

Fort Clatsop National Memorial Park is located in Oregon. The park includes a reconstruction of Lewis and Clark's winter fort.

Voyage Results

Lewis and Clark's grand expedition lasted more than two years. It was the first to cross America's unexplored West, taking the Corps on an 8,000-mile (12,900-km) journey!

Lewis and Clark returned with detailed maps and journals. They had gathered information about nearly 200 new plants. They had noted more than 100 new animals. And, they had learned about a variety of native tribes.

Following the expedition, Lewis became governor of the Louisiana Territory in 1807. He died on October 11, 1809, in Tennessee.

Clark settled in St. Louis. There, he participated in the fur trade and the **real estate** market. In 1808, he married Julia Hancock. The couple had five children together.

Beginning in 1813, Clark served four terms as governor of the Missouri Territory. When Julia died in 1820, William married Harriet Kennerly Radford. William Clark died in St. Louis on September 1, 1838.

1812	1856
Sacagawea died	Robert Edwin Peary born

1809	1838	1881
Lewis died	Clark died	Peary entered the U.S. Navy

Lewis and Clark returned to Missouri as heroes. Their maps and detailed journals inspired settlers to move West.

Today, Lewis and Clark are remembered for their contributions to the expansion of the United States. Their expedition allowed the country to claim the Oregon region. This included present-day Oregon, Washington, and Idaho. Soon, the United States stretched from the Atlantic Ocean to the Pacific Ocean.

1893
Peary's first expedition

1909
Peary's third expedition, reached the North Pole

1905
Peary's second expedition

1920
Peary died

Glossary

allies - people or countries that agree to help each other in times of need.

descend - to move from a higher place to a lower one.

embark - to make a start.

forage - to search.

geology - the science of Earth and its structure.

keelboat - a shallow, covered riverboat that is usually rowed, poled, or towed. A keelboat is used to carry cargo.

pirogue - a boat made by hollowing out a large log.

rapid - a fast-moving part of a river. Rocks or logs often break the surface of the water in this area.

real estate - property, which includes buildings and land.

recruit - to get someone to join a group.

Revolutionary War - from 1775 to 1783. A war for independence between Britain and its North American colonies. The colonists won and created the United States of America.

terrain - the physical features of an area of land. Mountains, rivers, and canyons can all be part of a terrain.

Saying It

Hidatsa - hih-DAHT-suh
Missoula - muh-ZOO-luh
Nez Percé - NEHZ PUHRS
pirogue - PEE-rohg
Sacagawea - sak-uh-juh-WEE-uh
Shoshone - shuh-SHOHN
Toussaint Charbonneau - too-san shawr-baw-noh

Web Sites

To learn more about Meriwether Lewis and William Clark, visit ABDO Publishing Company on the World Wide Web at **www.abdopublishing.com**. Web sites about Lewis and Clark are featured on our Book Links page. These links are routinely monitored and updated to provide the most current information available.

Index